Word Sk

This book belongs to

_____

Word
Fun

Name_____

Word Fun

Circle the words that match the pictures.

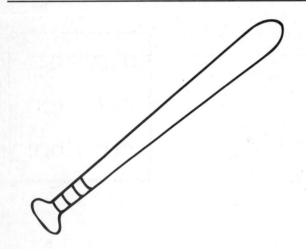

the	will
bat	bat
a	bat

Color the bat red.

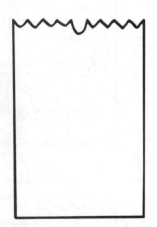

bag	fish
cat	bag
bag	A

Color the bag yellow.

FS109028 Word Skills

Name _____

I Can Read

Circle the words that match the pictures.

dog	hat
hat	top
cat	hat

Color the hat red.

sun	sun
fat	car
will	sun

Color the sun yellow.

3
reproducible

FS109028 Word Skills

Name _____

Color Words

Color two frogs green.
Color three fish orange.

Name _____

More Color Words

Color the dog brown.
Color one ball purple.
Color the flowers red.

FS109028 Word Skills

Name_____

Color the Cats

Color one cat black.
Color one cat brown.
Color one cat orange.

Name _____

Fun with Fish

Color five fish orange.
Color two fish blue.

FS109028 Word Skills

Name _____

Read and Color

Draw four yellow flowers.

Draw three purple presents.

Word Match

Match each word with a picture.

cat •

dog •

pan •

ball •

FS109028 Word Skills

Fun Word Match

Match each word with a picture.

jet •

leaf •

bed •

nut •

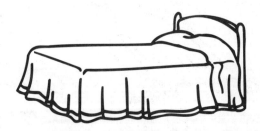

Opposites

Color the pictures. Draw a line from each word to the correct picture.

big

little

red

blue

big

little

yellow

green

big

little

blue

orange

Matching Words

Circle matching pairs of words.

go	go	sat	cat
fox	fox	at	to
top	toe	red	red
no	no	car	cat

Name _____

Rhyme Time

In each row, circle the things that rhyme.

FS109028 Word Skills

Rhyme Match

In each row, circle the thing that rhymes with the picture.

Name _____

Beginning Sounds

Write the beginning sound for each word.

Name _____

More Beginning Sounds

Write the beginning sound for each word.

at	ug	um
un	ag	us
an	ed	ox

Name _____

Write the Sounds

Write the beginning sound for each word.

_ o x	_ o p	_ u t
_ e g	_ a p	_ e n
_ a n	_ a t	_ e b

FS109028 Word Skills

Name _____

Ending Sounds

Write the ending sound for each word.

je

di

ba

pi

ru

bu

mo

ca

fo

FS109028 Word Skills

Name _____

More Ending Sounds

Write the ending sound for each word.

bi   ma   cu

pi   mo   to

be   si   da

19
reproducible

FS109028 Word Skills

Name _____

Making New Words

Color the picture. Add the letter. Write the word.

	c _a t_	
	p _a t_	
	h _a t_	
	r _a t_	

New Words

Color the picture. Add the letter. Write the word.

	p	
	ick	
	l	
	ick	
	k	
	ick	
	s	
	ick	

Add a Letter

Add each letter to make a word. Draw a line from each word to its picture.

p   d   w   b

_____
_ _ _ ig

_____
_ _ _ ig

_____
_ _ _ ig

_____
_ _ _ ig

FS109028 Word Skills

Adding Letters

Add each letter to make a word. Draw a line from each word to its picture.

h   **m**   **b**   **r**

_____ ug

_____ ug

_____ ug

_____ ug

FS109028 Word Skills

Rhyme Time

Match each word with a picture.

truck •

duck •

rat •

bat •

24
reproducible

FS109028 Word Skills

Name _____

 # Going on a Trip

Where would you like to go on a trip? Draw it.
Trace and finish the sentence.

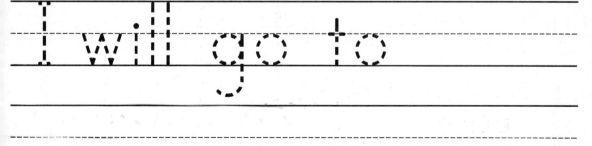

I will go to

25
reproducible

FS109028 Word Skills

Name _____

A Good Book

Think about a good book.
Write its name.

_____

- -

_____

Draw a picture about your book.

Name _____

I Have a Friend!

Write a word to complete each sentence.

_____

My friend's name is _____ .

_____

We like to play _____ .

_____

We like to eat _____ .

Draw a picture of you and your friend.

Playground Fun

Trace the words.

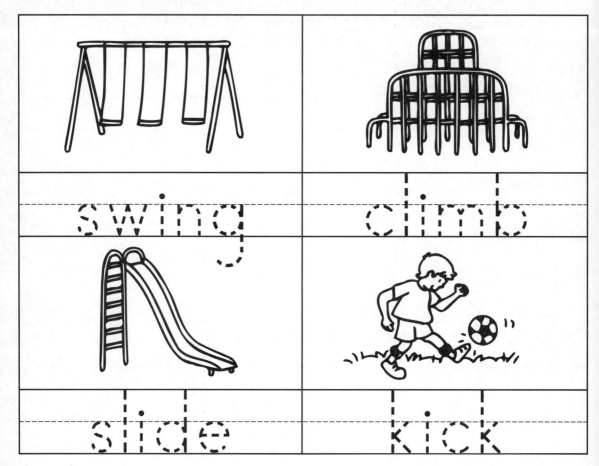

swing

climb

slide

kick

What do you like to do at the playground?

_____

- -

_____

Preparation

Remove the game board and the game cards from the center of the book. Cut out the game cards. Provide a game piece for each player.

How to Play

One or more children can play this game. The children place the game cards facedown in a stack and place their game pieces on START. The first player draws a card, reads it, and moves his or her game piece to the next space with the same shape that is on the game card. Return the card to the bottom of the stack. Then the next player takes a turn. Play continues until someone wins by reaching FINISH.

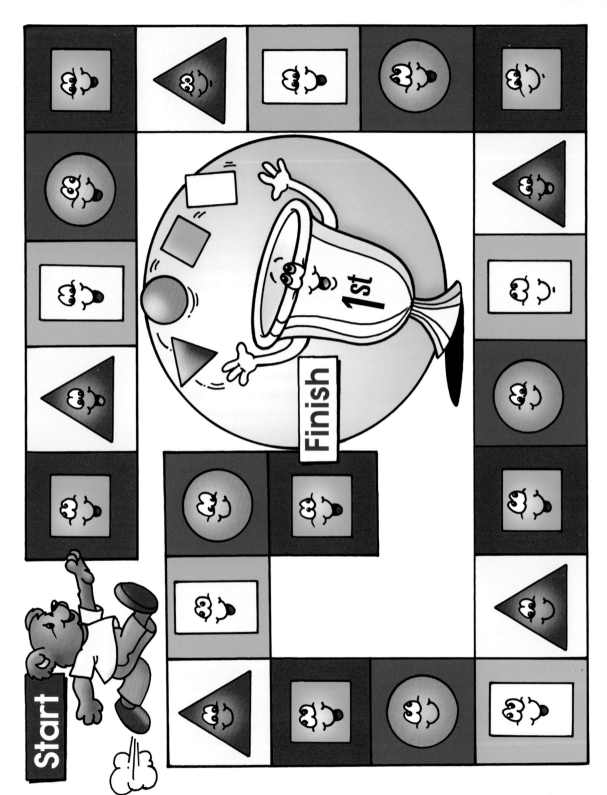

Start

Finish

1st

B

We are here. □

A cat is on the bed. ▲

Write your name. ■

They will go. ●

Give it to me. □

See him run. ▲

I see a dog. ▲

He makes a cake. ■

Do you have one? ●

The hat is red. ■

She can jump. ●

What time is it? □

C

D

Name _____

Writing Sentences

Write a word to complete each sentence.

_____

I can _____.

_____

I will _____.

_____

I see a _____.

_____

I cannot _____.

29
reproducible

FS109028 Word Skills

Name _____

Jack and Jill

Write the words where they belong.

up   and   to   a   and   came   his

_____   _____

Jack _____ Jill went _____ the hill

_____   _____

_____ fetch _____ pail of water.

_____   _____

Jack fell down _____ broke _____

_____

crown, and Jill _____ tumbling after.

30
reproducible   FS109028 Word Skills

Name _____

Humpty Dumpty

Write the words where they belong.

a   sat   had   the   fall   and   put   men

_____   _____

Humpty Dumpty _____ on _____ wall.

_____   _____

Humpty Dumpty _____ a great _____ .

_____   _____

All _____ king's horses _____ all the

_____   _____

king's _____ couldn't _____

Humpty together again.

FS109028 Word Skills

Name _____

Twinkle, Twinkle, Little Star

Write the words where they belong.

star   you   I   the   a   so   little   the

_____   _____

Twinkle, twinkle, little _____ . How _____

_____

wonder what _____ are. Up above

_____   _____   _____

_____ world _____ high. Like _____

_____

diamond in _____ sky. Twinkle, twinkle,

_____

_____ star. How I wonder what you are.

32
reproducible   FS109028 Word Skills

Name _____

Happy Birthday

Write the words where they belong.

to   you   birthday   'Happy   _____

your name

_____
- - - - - - - - - - - - - - - - -

Happy birthday _____ you.

_____
- -

Happy _____ to you.

_____
- -

Happy birthday, dear _____.

_____   _____
- - - - - - - - - - - - - -   - - - - - - - - - - - - - -

_____ birthday to _____.

Name _____

Reading Signs

Read each sign. Draw a line to the matching picture.

Go to a
school.

Go to
a park.

Go to
a zoo.

FS109028 Word Skills

Let's Eat Breakfast!

Read each sentence. Draw a line to the matching picture.

I will eat a pancake.

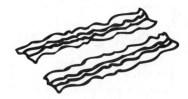

I will eat a waffle.

I will eat cereal.

I will eat bacon.

Let's Eat Lunch!

Read each sentence. Draw a line to the matching picture.

I will eat a sandwich.

I will eat a banana.

I will eat chips.

I will eat a cookie.

Name _____

Let's Eat Dinner!

Read each sentence. Draw a line to the matching picture.

I will eat spaghetti.

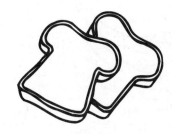

I will eat green beans.

I will eat bread.

I will eat a cupcake.

FS109028 Word Skills

Name _____

I Like Fruit!

Finish each sentence with the name of a fruit.

bananas

apples

grapes

pears

_____
- -
I like _____.

_____
- -
I like _____.

_____
- -
I like _____.

_____
- -
I like _____.

Name _____

The Zoo

Finish each sentence with the name of an animal.

bear

monkey

snake

zebra

_____

I see a _____.

I see a _____.

I see a _____.

I see a _____.

FS109028 Word Skills

A Classroom

Finish each sentence with the name of what you see.

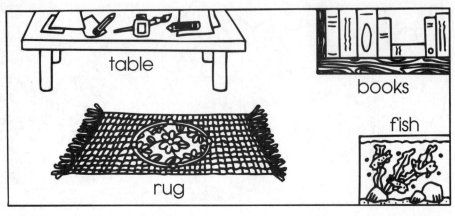

table

books

fish

rug

_____

You will go to the _____ .

_____

You will go to the _____ .

_____

You will go to the _____ .

_____

You will go to the _____ .

FS109028 Word Skills

Name _____

All about Me

The color of my eyes is
_____

- - - - - - - - - - - - - - - - - - -
_____ .

The color of my hair is
_____

- - - - - - - - - - - - - - - - - - -
_____ .

I look like this:

My Favorite Foods

_____   _____
- - - - - - - - - - - - - -   - - - - - - - - - - - - - -
_____   _____

_____   _____
- - - - - - - - - - - - - -   - - - - - - - - - - - - - -
_____   _____

41
reproducible

FS109028 Word Skills

Name _____

My Favorite Colors

Use your two favorite colors to fill in the spots.

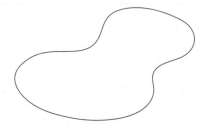 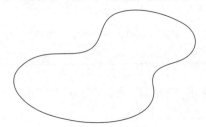

My two favorite colors are

_____   _____

- - - - - - - - - - - - - - - - - - -   - - - - - - - - - - - - - - - - - - -

_____ and _____.

My Favorite Toys

Draw two favorite toys.

My two favorite toys are

_____   _____

- - - - - - - - - - - - - - - - - - -   - - - - - - - - - - - - - - - - - - -

_____ and _____.

FS109028 Word Skills

Name _____

All about My Family

Draw your family.

_____

- - - - - - - - - - - - - - - - -

I have _____ people in my family.

_____

My Favorite Animals

Draw two favorite animals.

My two favorite animals are

_____   _____

- - - - - - - - - - - - - - -   - - - - - - - - - - - - - - -

a _____ and a _____.

Words

Write the correct word on each line.

I will go to a _____

_____

_____ .

pond

pool

We need some _____

_____

_____ .

food

rocks

I want to read a _____

_____

_____ .

menu

book

I can help the _____

_____

_____ .

cat

dog

Name _____

Animal Names

Write the animal's name on each line.

bear

pig

frog

horse

_____
- -
_____

_____
- -
_____

_____
- -
_____

_____
- -
_____

Name _____

What Happens Next?

Look at the pictures. Write the sentences.

Will she go in the pool?

1. _____ ?

She will go in the pool.

2. _____ .

FS109028 Word Skills

Name _____

What Is Next?

Look at the pictures. Write the sentences.

He is in the wagon.

_____
- -
1. _____ .

It will not go.

_____
- -
2. _____ .

FS109028 Word Skills

Name _____

At the Park

Look at the picture. Find 3 living things.
Write their names.

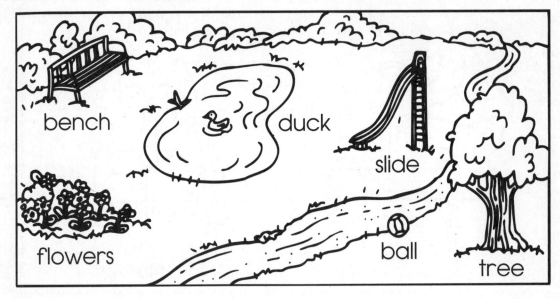

bench duck slide

flowers ball tree

1. _____

2. _____

3. _____

FS109028 Word Skills

Name _____

At the Beach

Look at the picture. Find 3 living things.
Write their names.

1. _____

2. _____

3. _____

Name _____

In the Forest

Look at the picture. Find 3 living things.
Write their names.

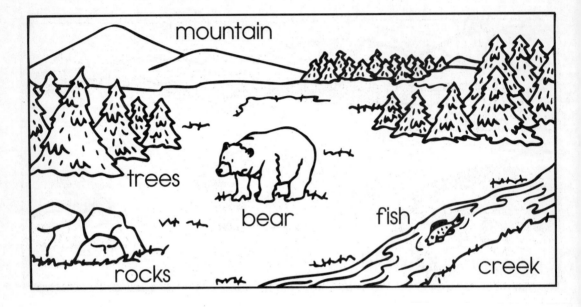

mountain

trees

bear

fish

rocks

creek

_____

1. _____

2. _____

3. _____

Name _____

At the Farm

Look at the picture. Find 3 living things.
Write their names.

1. _____

2. _____

3. _____

FS109028 Word Skills

At the Market

Look at the picture. Find 3 foods. Write their names.

1. _____

2. _____

3. _____

Name _____

A Busy Street

Look at the picture. Write 3 things that people ride.

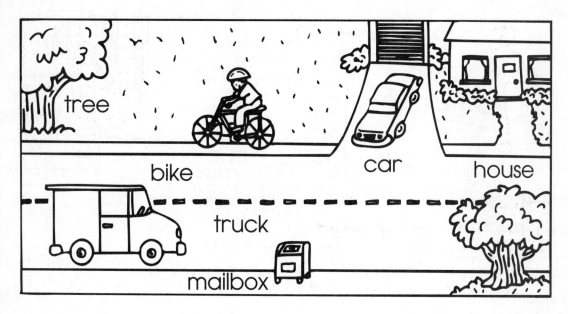

tree

bike

car

house

truck

mailbox

1. _____

2. _____

3. _____

FS109028 Word Skills

Name _____

My Toy

I put a bear in my toy box.

I put a ball in my toy box.

I put a dinosaur in my toy box.

What would you put in your toy box?

Draw it.

Write it.

_____

- -

_____

My Lunch Box

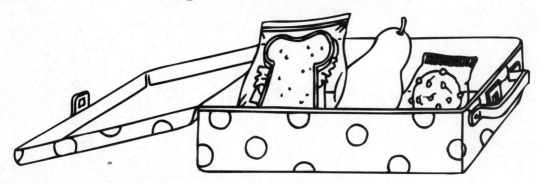

I put a sandwich in my lunch box.

I put a pear in my lunch box.

I put a cookie in my lunch box.

What would you put in your lunch box?
Draw it.

Write it.

_____

is wonderful with words!

_____
signature

_____
date

56
reproducible